MW01253297

THE UNOFFICIAL *FORTNITE*®
SURVIVAL GUIDE

PLAYING NICE WITH OTHERS IN *FORTNITE*®

RAY STERN

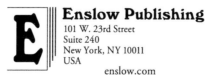

Enslow Publishing
101 W. 23rd Street
Suite 240
New York, NY 10011
USA
enslow.com

Published in 2020 by Enslow Publishing, LLC
101 W. 23rd Street, Suite 240, New York, NY 10011

Library of Congress Cataloging-in-Publication Data

Names: Stern, Ray.
Title: Playing nice with others in Fortnite® / Ray Stern.
Description: New York : Enslow Publishing, 2020. | Series: The unofficial Fortnite® survival guide | Includes glossary and index.
Identifiers: ISBN 9781978517271 (pbk.) | ISBN 9781978517295 (library bound) | ISBN 9781978517288 (6 pack)
Subjects: LCSH: Fortnite Battle Royale (Game)--Juvenile literature. | Imaginary wars and battles--Juvenile literature. | Video games--Juvenile literature.
Classification: LCC GV1469.35.F67 S874 2020 | DDC 794.8--dc23

Printed in the United States of America

CONTENTS

INTRODUCTION

It's been insanely popular since the day it was released, and its dance moves have taken the world by storm. You already know what game is being described here, and that game is *Fortnite*, of course. It takes the best parts of shooters and the best parts of building and resources games and smashes them together in a competitive, fast-paced game where you have to beat out as many as ninety-nine other players and use the whole environment around you to survive. But you know what's even better than you against the world? You and your buddies against the world!

Fortnite: Battle Royale offers various ways to play based on how many teammates you have. As mentioned, you can take everyone on and be just you against the world for the next twenty minutes, but it's been noted that *Fortnite*'s true surprise element is how nice its community is to one another. There's no need to go it alone if you don't have to! Take a cue from the different

team modes and learn how rewarding watching someone else's back can be. Through the forts you build, the traps you set, and the dances you bust out, *Fortnite* turns you into a lean, but

Keep your friends just as close as your foes in a battle royale for maximum success.

not too mean, fighting machine. However, the best fort you build will be the friends you make along the way.

It's important to note, though, that if you don't have real-life friends who'll be joining you in the game, random players will be assigned to your team. It's a great way to meet new people, but always remember to be careful about what personal information you might be sharing. No matter how cool or nice someone seems, a stranger is still a stranger, and it's best to keep these kinds of friendships to the game map only.

CHAPTER 1

Friends, Not Foes

When choosing your team format, it's good to know what the differences in modes are and how many teammates will be joining you. You have a choice among duos, squads, or the extremely popular 50 v. 50 play.

Duos

The duos mode is the best way to play with a buddy. The two players can team up to build, attack, or to play lookout for one while the other is taking action. It's recommended that the two players stick

The duos mode gives you and your best buddy the chance to bond even more.

together. The number-one rule of advice in dealing with duos is to take out individuals who have separated from their partners. So try not to separate! It's much easier to get picked off that way.

Anyone who does get injured doesn't "die" right away, as they would in solo play. A partner can revive and heal a fallen friend. It's best to find a pal who is more skilled in an area that you're not so great at. Covering a friend who's great at building forts for both of you is a good plan. If the duo can stay together, they will have an automatic advantage over duos who split up. Once one teammate is down, the duo is in danger, so be sure to cover each other.

Squads

Squads give players the best chance to lean into their specific strengths. Builder, sniper, scout, and coordinator are all important roles. Someone who has fast reflexes and mastery of their controls can be a great scout, going slightly ahead of the group in order to scope out the map in play. Someone who prefers the building aspect of *Fortnite* can enjoy the benefits of

Squad goals: Keep an eye on that compass and coordinate your team! Then dance it out.

teammates protecting him or her as he or she constructs the structures as necessary.

Someone who's got a good eye for details and is a little bossy will be great at coordinating the team by keeping watch over the compass. And someone who's both patient and one step ahead of others can be a great sniper, anticipating where an opponent will sprint to next. By working together, squads build trust and sharpen one another's game.

THE ART OF GOOD SPORTSMANSHIP

Gaming culture does have one bad stereotype attached to it: the reputation of mean and nasty gamers. *Fortnite* has done much to build a community that is invested in helping one another succeed:

- **Always congratulate your allies for a job well done.** Even a team loss will have positive moments worth recognizing.
- **Remember that the odds are against you!** A Victory Royale is very hard to achieve. No one should feel bad about losing.
- **Even your opponents are worth applauding.** You may hate dying when your cool structure is blown up but check out how great their dance moves are.
- **You will have another shot.** What can you do differently in the next round?

Remember, you were also new to this game once. It can feel awesome when you win, but lift your opponent up, too.

50 v. 50

In 50 v. 50, players are broken up into two teams, which means the goal is to destroy only half of the other players, not all of them, and to come out the top scorer against your allies. In many ways, 50 v. 50 is peak *Fortnite*. A player has a lot of allies for backup, but he or she can still experience a feeling of playing

The 50 v. 50 mode is great for those who like to do their own thing but with backup.

solo, just with a sense of security supporting his or her game.

This mode seems to encourage the most generosity in players as well. Nick Statt noted in an article on *The Verge* that "players seem to go out of their way to assist strangers…50 v. 50 incentivizes players to revive complete strangers, gift weapons…and otherwise be a nice human being and solid team player." There's also a 20 v. 20 mode, with fewer players and smaller teams.

CHAPTER 2

Gaming the System

*F*ortnite puts a unique spin on shooter-style games. It's not enough to know how to run and shoot opponents. It's not enough to know how to harvest resources for building. The key to the game is how one can combine the two while also coordinating with any possible allies. Also, those sweet, sweet dance moves.

Find Your Role

Fortnite brings together so many different elements that it can be overwhelming to play at first. However, it gives players the opportunity to lean into their personal strengths as well. When playing in a squad, for instance, it's recommended that there be only two members building at any one time. This leaves room for other players

When you find your niche in *Fortnite*'s world, you can elevate your whole squad's performance.

to scout out vulnerable opponents and coordinate strategies.

A builder needs a good imagination and strategic planning. How high should one build a structure? Is height more important or a solid foundation? How many ramps will go inside? Can resources be harvested discretely? A builder has the mind of a puzzles enthusiast.

A scout has the ability to sneak around, to dodge and weave, and to jump out of the line of fire. A scout can spot chests, abandoned loot and resources, and vulnerable opponents. This role is great for someone who loves to charge in and stay on the move.

A sniper is alert and responsible for keeping the perimeter secure. Sniper rifles are mainly projectile weapons, which means the shots will take a little while to travel across the distance fired. Therefore, a sniper needs to anticipate opponents' movements. A sniper should also have great hearing and an eye for detail to scope out more hidden opponents.

There is room for a player who is good at all tasks. Such a player is versatile and can move into different roles as needed. Maybe he or she can build, then switch to scouting ahead. Maybe he or she can carry all the health and revive potions. The opportunities are as flexible as the gameplay.

It's great to be a flexible and versatile player. Those who rule all roles can rule Battle Royale!

WHAT'S THE FORECAST?

The biggest opponent in *Fortnite* is the Storm, a weather phenomenon meant to push players out of hiding and into the fray. As the eye of the Storm shrinks, so does the safe play area. No weapon will defeat the Storm, and the damage it deals is bad. Getting caught outside the eye is something to avoid. Consider delegating storm-watch duties to an ally who will watch the clock closely and give updates on when the eye is about to shrink again. Some players will jump into the circle right before it closes in order to prevent being targets, but the most important thing is to get inside that circle!

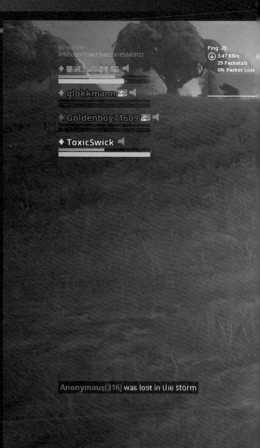

The Storm is the undefeatable opponent. It's hard to recover from damage caused by the Storm.

Communication Is Key

All your careful strategies will not pay off without communication. Ed Thorn, in an article on *Metabomb*, recommends using the time in the pregame lobby for planning. Even if it's just a quick go-round calling out your specialty, everyone on your team can know who's covering what on the map.

Another common tip is to land together. There's a bonus advantage to landing on a roof and going through the structure top to bottom. That way, weapons resources inside can be harvested as your squad goes through the building. But at the very least, land together. And if an area is hot, everyone needs to be on alert, ready to crouch and grab the first weapons available.

Whatever role you take on a team, be sure to relay opponents' movements through the compass. Try to keep spoken communication short. Talking too much can give away your position.

Sharing Is Caring

A successful team isn't just well practiced. A successful team also takes care of its members. *Fortnite*'s reputation of having a helpful, friendly community comes mainly from players willing to share their weapons, healing potions, and ammo. Often, players share because they are

Keeping a slot free will help you benefit from other players' generosity.

confident that whatever they're giving up to one ally will be returned to them by the generosity of another player. Naturally, there's a practical interest in keep allies healed and armed. And with only five slots for inventory, being able to constantly cycle through weapons and better revivals improves one's game, which in turn should improve everyone's game.

Sharing includes telling allies about loot or inventory one had to leave behind. Get in the habit of calling this out as you go—although don't yell this in a hot zone, of course.

CHAPTER 3

Problematic Players

*F*ortnite's gaming community is special compared to those of similar games, but there are still players who can ruin everyone's fun. Whether by malice, poor social skills, or incompetence, there are players who will test everyone else's patience.

Trolls Who Enjoy Ruining Things and How to Cope with Them

Dealing with a mean player happens to everyone. Don't let anyone ruin your experience!

It's a sad but true fact that there are players who enjoy playing the game at the expense of others' fun. To make it worse, the more others get upset at this player, the funnier the troll finds it to annoy others. A troll could be someone who intentionally sabotages his or her own team by giving away locations, not sharing resources, or refusing to watch anyone's back. More commonly, a troll will disrupt a temporary truce by trying to shoot everyone and take all the loot.

A troll can be a bully, calling other players nasty names in the chat. It's hard not to retaliate against such treatment, but it's usually best not to respond. Instead, report that player for using hateful speech. If necessary, leave the match or take a break from the game to cool off. Try to find friends and voices who can provide a counterbalance to the streams of negativity from a troll and give your focus to positive feedback as much as possible.

What to Do with the Weakest Link

Not everyone is a *Fortnite* expert. The best way to treat someone less competent is with patience and kindness. Find a way to share helpful tips,

SAFETY DANCE

The popularity of the dance emotes are a huge part of *Fortnite*'s success. A slick set of moves caught on video can go viral. As *Fortnite*'s map keeps getting updated, fun surprises, like secret dance floors, are added. These dance floors are generally used as safe spaces, where opponents can show off their moves to one another without fear of attack. If a troll crashes the party, it's common for the other players to temporarily team up to defend the sanctity of the dance floor.

whether by sending a less experienced player links to tutorials or by pointing out opponents in his or her vicinity. Try not to be bossy, though. No one likes being ordered around unless everyone has agreed that one person is in charge.

You can offer to let a less experienced player shadow you and give him or her helpful tasks. If you're a builder, a shadow can keep harvesting resources for you. At some point, the weakest link will be hit by an opponent. It's

Taking the time to learn from a more experienced player can improve your game. Appreciate her knowledge!

great to help keep a fallen ally alive by sharing some healing resources, but it's also okay to set a limit on how many times that player will be revived. And someone who refuses to accept his or her low skill level and ignores the team's strategies will eventually be left behind. Don't be afraid to put the team's welfare ahead of an individual's.

Oh No, I'm the Weakest Link!

It can feel really embarrassing to admit your skills need improvement. However, everyone has started out green at one point. All the experienced players learned, and so can you.

It's also helpful to remember that a Victory Royale is a long shot. Try setting different goals, like "I'm going to find a legendary weapon" or "I'm going to make it halfway through the clock." Taking pressure off oneself can definitely improve gameplay.

The 50 v. 50 mode can be a great learning environment for a new player. *Fortnite* pro Tyler "Ninja" Blevins likes to encourage players to charge in to hot zones and take their hits, but he also points out that landing on the far end of the island can give a player a chance to

Sometimes throwing yourself into the action is the best way to learn the game!

practice building. Shadowing willing and more experienced players is another option. And the recent addition of a Creative Mode has proven to be popular with players of all levels. It allows players to build and explore without running into danger along the way.

However you choose to improve, there are no shortage of tools to help you learn. But if it turns out that you're never going to be a legendary great player, all that really matters is having fun. As long as *Fortnite* is fun to play, you're always playing it right.

GLOSSARY

ALLY A friendly player on your team.

BUILDING The act of creating structures using harvested resources.

COMPASS One of the displays players can use to keep track of opponents and their movements.

DUO A team made up of two players.

EMOTE Special moves players can do to communicate, including dance moves.

EYE The center of the storm during the game; it shrinks throughout the match.

50 V. 50 One of the team play modes that splits the players into two teams of fifty.

LOBBY The area where players wait before starting a game; it's a good place to discuss strategy.

MODE One of the styles of gameplay, including solo, duo, or 50 v. 50.

OPPONENT An enemy player.

PLAYER An active participant in the game.

RAMP A platform a builder can construct to jump up on and travel around the terrain to get out of the way of opponents' fire.

REVIVE A potion a player can give to a downed ally for healing.

SHOOTER A video game where the goal is to shoot other players.

SOLO The individual mode that pits up to one hundred players against one another.

SPRINT The style of movement players do to run from one point to another on the map.

SQUAD A team made up of four players.

STORM The weather phenomenon that terrorizes players; they need to stay within the eye of the storm or risk suffering a lot of damage.

STRUCTURE A building created by the resources harvested in the game.

TROLL A player who enjoys being mean to other players or winning through unfair tactics.

TUTORIAL A video that explains how to play or improve certain skills.

20 V. 20 A variation on the 50 v. 50 play mode that pits five teams of twenty players each against one another.

FOR MORE INFORMATION

Entertainment Software Rating Board
Website: http://www.esrb.org

Fortnite, Epic Games, Inc.
Website: https://www.epicgames.com/fortnite/en-US/home

iD Tech
Website: https://www.idtech.com

International Game Developers Association – Toronto
Website: https://www.igda.org/members/group

Team Ninja
Website: http://www.teamninja.com

We Got Game!
Website: http://wegotgame.ca

FOR FURTHER READING

Abbott, Josh. Fortnite, *Android, Mac, IOS, Xbox One, PC, Windows, Apk, Unblocked, Guide*. Oxford, UL: Gamer Guides, LLC, 2018.

Amodio, Louise. Fortnite: Battle Royale: *Mini Guide and Gaming Notebook for Epic Fortniters*. New York, NY: Beans and Joy Publishing Ltd., 2018.

Bossom, Andy, and Ben Dunning. *Video Games: An Introduction to the Industry*. New York, NY: Fairchild Books, 2016.

Epic Games. Fortnite *(Official): Battle Royale Survival Guide*. New York, NY: Little, Brown Books, 2019.

Epic Games. Fortnite *(Official) 2020 Calendar*. New York, NY: Hachette, 2018.

HSE Guides. Fortnite *Game, Battle Royale, Download, Ps4, Tips, Multiplayer, Guide Unofficial*. Oxford, UK: Gamer Guides, LLC, 2018.

Kuhn, Damien. *The* Fortnite *Guide to Staying Alive: Tips and Tricks for Every Kind of Player*. Kansas City, MO: Andrews McMeel Publishing, 2018.

Rich, Jason R. *An Encyclopedia of Strategy for Fortniters: An Unofficial Guide for Battle Royale*. London, UK: Studio Press, 2018.

St. Victor, Josiah. Fortnite *Full Pro Guide*. CreateSpace Independent Publishing, 2018.

INDEX

About the Author

Ray Stern is from Colorado and has the dopest dance moves in town.

Photo Credits

Cover Ben Gingell/Shutterstock.com; pp. 4–5 Bartosz Siedlik/AFP/Getty Images; p. 7 Adam Crowley/Getty Images; p. 10 Colorblind Images LLC/DigitalVision/Getty Images; p. 11 SAHACHATZ/Shutterstock.com; p. 21 SG SHOT/ Shutterstock.com; p. 24 (left) Maskot/Getty Images; pp. 24–25 © iStockphoto.com/g-stockstudio.

Design & Layout: Brian Garvey; Editor: Bethany Bryan; Photo Researcher: Nicole DiMella; *Fortnite* Consultant: Sam Keppeler